DINOSAUR WORLD

Long Arm
The Adventure of Brachiosaurus

Written by Michael Dahl

Illustrated by Garry Nichols

Special thanks to our advisers for their expertise:

Content Adviser: Philip J. Currie, Curator of Dinosaurs,
Royal Tyrrell Museum of Palaeontology, Drumheller, Alberta, Canada

Reading Adviser: Susan Kesselring, M.A., Literacy Educator,
Rosemount - Apple Valley - Eagan (Minnesota) School District

PICTURE WINDOW BOOKS
Minneapolis, Minnesota

Managing Editor: Catherine Neitge
Creative Director: Terri Foley
Art Director: Keith Griffin
Editor: Patricia Stockland
Designer: Joe Anderson
Page production: Picture Window Books
The illustrations in this book were prepared digitally.

Picture Window Books
5115 Excelsior Boulevard
Suite 232
Minneapolis, MN 55416
877-845-8392
www.picturewindowbooks.com

Printed in the United States of America.

Library of Congress Cataloging-in-Publication Data
Dahl, Michael.
Long arm : the adventure of Brachiosaurus / written by
Michael Dahl ; illustrated by Garry Nichols.
p. cm. — (Dinosaur world)
Includes bibliographical references and index.
ISBN 1-4048-0939-2 (hardcover)
ISBN 1-4048-1835-9 (paperback)
1. Brachiosaurus—Juvenile literature. I. Nichols, Garry,
1958- ill. II. Title.

QE862.S3D295 2005
567.913—dc22
                             2004018576

No humans lived during the time of the dinosaurs. No person heard them roar, saw their scales, or felt their feathers.

The giant creatures are gone, but their fossils, or remains, lie hidden in the earth. Dinosaur skulls, skeletons, and eggs have been buried in rock for millions of years.

All around the world, scientists dig up fossils and carefully study them. Bones show how tall the dinosaurs stood. Claws and teeth show how they grabbed and what they ate. Scientists compare fossils with the bodies of living creatures such as birds and reptiles, which are relatives of the dinosaurs. Every year, scientists learn more and more about the giants that have disappeared.

Studying fossils and figuring out how the dinosaurs lived is like putting together the pieces of a puzzle that is millions of years old.

This is what some of those pieces can tell us about the dinosaur known as *Brachiosaurus* (BRA-kee-o-SOR-us).

The morning sun peeked over the edge of the horizon. Soft, pink sunlight touched the leafy branches.

The treetops shivered. The leaves began to shake. Something big was moving below.

Up popped a strange-looking head. *Brachiosaurus* stretched its snout high into the air.

Brachiosaurus's long neck helped it find tasty leaves other creatures couldn't reach.

Brachiosaurus's neck bones were hollow and light. This allowed the creature to easily move its head up and down. Besides being one of the tallest, *Brachiosaurus* was also one of the largest land animals to live on Earth. The creature's mighty body stretched longer than two city buses parked end to end.

Brachiosaurus's head pushed up through the treetops. The mighty creature blinked in the bright sunlight. Then it opened its toothy jaws and ripped the leaves from the closest tree branch.

Brachiosaurus was an herbivore, a plant-eating dinosaur. Its 52 teeth were shaped like long, flat spoons. *Brachiosaurus* could strip leaves off a tree, but it could not chew them. The dinosaur swallowed whole leaves and twigs down its long, wide throat.

Brachiosaurus lowered its head. Its long neck stretched over ferns and past tree trunks.

Brachiosaurus scooped up a small pile of stones off the ground. It swallowed the stones.

Since *Brachiosaurus* could not chew its food, the dinosaur swallowed stones to help grind up food already inside its stomach. Scientists call these stones gastroliths. Some gastroliths were the size of peanuts. Others were the size of human fists.

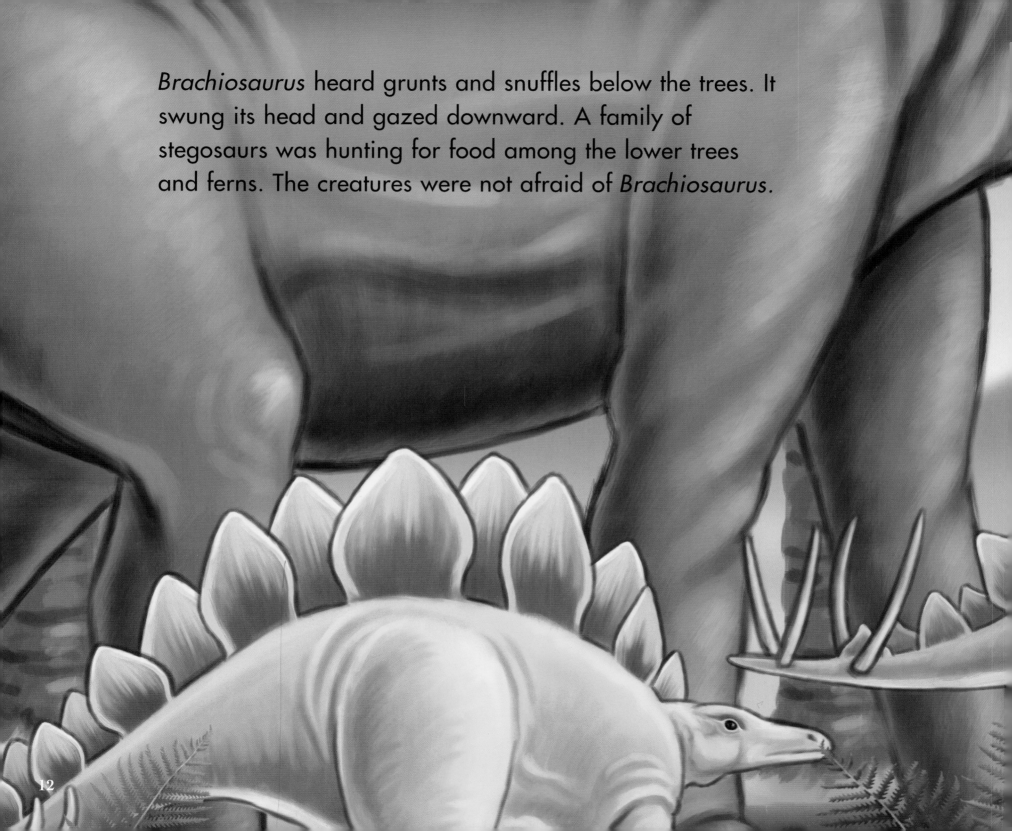

Brachiosaurus heard grunts and snuffles below the trees. It swung its head and gazed downward. A family of stegosaurs was hunting for food among the lower trees and ferns. The creatures were not afraid of *Brachiosaurus*.

They calmly plodded past the tall legs. Giant *Brachiosaurus* ignored the smaller creatures and went back to feeding from the treetops.

Unlike most land dinosaurs, *Brachiosaurus*'s front legs were taller than its back legs. *Brachiosaurus* means "arm lizard." The dinosaur was so tall that a stegosaur could crawl between its legs without scraping its bony back on *Brachiosaurus*'s belly!

13

As *Brachiosaurus* moved to feed on another tree, it saw a tall neck swaying in the distance.

Brachiosaurus lifted its snout and bellowed a greeting.
Its long-necked cousin roared back from far away.

Brachiosaurus was a type of dinosaur
known as a sauropod. Sauropods
looked like giant lizards with long
necks and tails. Scientists believe that
Brachiosaurus, like other sauropods,
traveled and fed in small herds.

Brachiosaurus sniffed the air. The other sauropods were also busy snuffling with their snouts. Water was close by.

The mighty creatures plodded away from the forest. Nearby, in a swampy field, *Brachiosaurus* saw a wide, shallow river.

Brachiosaurus stretched its neck far over the swamp plants and muddy shore. Then it plunged its head into the river. While it drank, the nose holes on top of its skull sniffed for danger.

Scientists used to think that *Brachiosaurus* was a water dinosaur and spent most of its time wading through rivers and lakes. But *Brachiosaurus* could weigh as much as 20 elephants. Scientists realized that *Brachiosaurus* would sink in soft sand. Scientists now believe that *Brachiosaurus* spent its time on land.

Brachiosaurus lifted its head and saw a fearsome shape on the other side of the water. Allosaurus stood on the riverbank. The meat-eater flashed its terrible teeth and roared.

Brachiosaurus stared at the deadly predator. Then it slowly lifted its head up, up, up.

Brachiosaurus towered far above its enemy. *Allosaurus* arched its neck as it looked at the powerful back and tail of *Brachiosaurus*. The hungry meat-eater roared again and turned away.

Brachiosaurus's immense size and height protected it from carnivores, or meat-eaters, like *Allosaurus*. Scientists believe that when creatures threatened younger and smaller sauropods, the adults would form a wall around them, shielding them from danger.

Brachiosaurus lumbered slowly back to the forest. There were more tasty leaves to eat before the end of the day.

Brachiosaurus: Where ...

Brachiosaurus fossils have been found in the United States—western Colorado, Wyoming, and Utah.

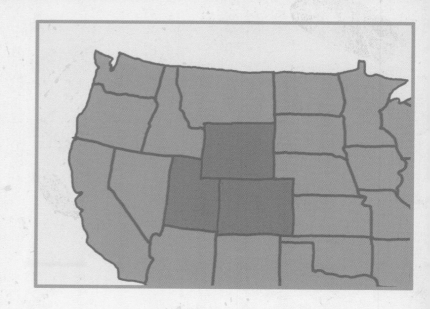

... and When

The "Age of Dinosaurs" began 248 million years ago (mya). If we imagine the time from the beginning of the dinosaur age to the present as one day, the Age of Dinosaurs lasted 18 hours—and humans have only been around for 10 minutes!

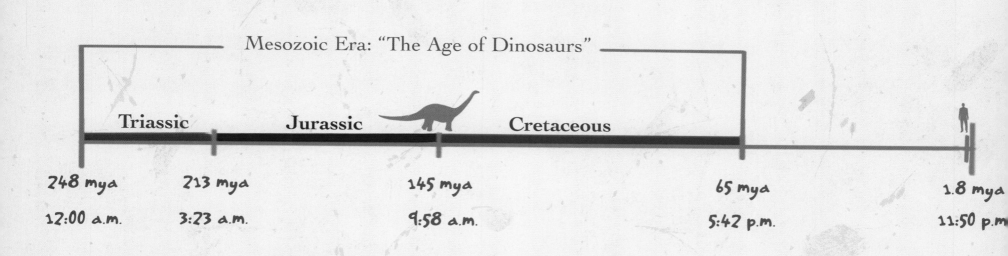

Mesozoic Era: "The Age of Dinosaurs"

Triassic   Jurassic   Cretaceous

248 mya	213 mya	145 mya	65 mya	1.8 mya
12:00 a.m.	3:23 a.m.	9:58 a.m.	5:42 p.m.	11:50 p.m.

Triassic—Dinosaurs first appear. Early mammals appear.
Jurassic—First birds appear.
Cretaceous—Flowering plants appear. By the end of this era, all dinosaurs disappear.

—First humans appear

—*Brachiosaurus* lived

Digging Deeper

High and Hollow

Brachiosaurus was more than twice the size of most predators of the time, such as *Allosaurus*, *Ceratosaurus*, and *Torvosaurus*. Its huge neck towered over the meat-eaters. The backbones of *Brachiosaurus* had small holes in their sides. These holes were filled with air sacs. The air sacs made the gigantic neck light enough to move up and down.

How High?

Brachiosaurus was one of the world's tallest dinosaurs. Its neck towered more than 50 feet above the ground, the height of a five-story building.

Giraffe Giant

Brachiosaurus is one of the very few dinosaurs whose front legs were longer than its back legs. Most four-footed dinosaurs had bodies that sloped forward toward their heads. *Brachiosaurus* had a high back that sloped down to its tail. The tall front legs gave *Brachiosaurus* a stance like a modern-day giraffe.

Full Tummy

Brachiosaurus spent most of its waking hours eating and hunting for food. Some scientists think that in order to keep its gigantic body healthy and in working order, *Brachiosaurus* had to eat hundreds of pounds of food each day! Its gut was always full of plant leaves, branches, and tree needles being ground up by gastroliths and dissolved by digestive juices.

Words to Know

carnivore — a creature that eats only meat, or other living creatures

dinosaurs — giant creatures that lived millions of years ago; scientists think that many modern reptiles and birds are related to dinosaurs

herbivore — a creature that eats only plants

gastrolith — stomach stones; rocks and pebbles inside a dinosaur's stomach help grind up its food

sauropod — a special type of dinosaur; sauropods are plant-eaters; they look like gigantic lizards, have long tails, long necks, and walk on four tree trunk-like legs

To Learn More

At the Library

Cohen, Daniel. *Brachiosaurus*. Mankato, Minn.: Bridgestone Books, 2003.

Matthews, Rupert. *Brachiosaurus*. Chicago: Heinemann Library, 2003.

Oliver, Rupert. *Brachiosaurus*. Vero Beach, Fla.: Rourke Publishing, 2001.

On the Web

FactHound offers a safe, fun way to find Web sites related to this book. All of the sites on FactHound have been researched by our staff. *www.facthound.com*

1. Visit the FactHound home page.
2. Enter a search word related to this book, or type in this special code: 1404809392
3. Click on the FETCH IT button.

Your trusty FactHound will fetch the best Web sites for you!